JOURNEYS

Reader's Notebook
Volume 1

Grade 1

HOUGHTON MIFFLIN HARCOURT
School Publishers

Printed in the U.S.A.

ISBN   978-0-547-86060-2

28 29 30   0928   21 20 19 18

4500709853   B C D E F G

Contents

Listen for the Short *a* and *m* Sounds

 Say each picture name. Listen for the short a sound. Write the letter **a** to show where you hear the short a sound.

1.	2.	3.

_ _ _ _ ▮	_ _ _ _ ▮	_ _ _ _ ▮

 Say each picture name. Listen for the *m* sound. Write the letter **m** to show where you hear the sound for **m**.

4.	5.	6.

_ _ ▮ _ _	_ _ ▮ _ _	_ _ ▮ _ _

Name _____

Words to Know

✏️ Read the words in the box. Then read and finish the sentences.

•••••••••••••• **Words to Know** ••••••••••••••

am   I   to   like

••

_____

I am _____ .

_____

I like to _____ .

🖍️ Draw a picture to go with your sentences.

Listen for the *s*, *m*, and Short *a* Sounds

✏️ Say each picture name. Listen for the /s/ sound. Write the letter **s** to show where you hear the sound for **s**.

1. 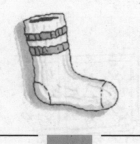	2. 	3. 

✏️ Listen to each picture name. Listen for the sounds. Use the letters **s**, **a**, or **m** to write the picture name. Remember that a person's name begins with a capital letter.

4. 	5. 	6. 
_ _ _ t	_ _ d	_ _ _

Words to Know

Read the words in the box. Then read the story.

Words to Know

a   see   the   I   to   like

I am Sam.

I see a .

I like the 🐶 .

I see a 🐱 .

I like the 🐱 .

✏️ Draw what will happen next in the story.

Name _____

Listen for the *t*, *s*, *m*, and Short *a* Sounds

✏️ Say each picture name. Listen for the *t* sound. Write the letter **t** to show where you hear the sound for **t**.

1.	2.	3.
		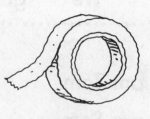

✏️ Listen to each picture name. Listen for the sounds. Use the letters **t, s, a,** or **m** to write the name.

4.	5.	6.
 ___ ___ p		

Words to Know

 Read the words in the box. Then read
the story. Draw a line under the words that
have short **a**.

> **Words to Know**
>
> we   go   I   a   see   like   to   the

I am Tam.

I am Sam.

We see a mat.

We like the mat.

We go to the mat.

 Draw what Sam and Tam will do next.

Name _____

Listen for the *c*, *t*, *m*, and Short *a* Sounds

Phonics

✏️ Say each picture name. Listen for the sounds in the name. Color the pictures that begin with the same sound as **cat**.

1.

✏️ Listen to each picture name. Listen for the sounds. Use the letters **c, t, a,** or **m** to write the picture name.

2.	3.	4.

_ _ p	_ _ n	_ _ _

Words to Know

Read the words in the box. Then read the story. Draw a line under the words that have short a.

Words to Know

is   are   we   go   I   a   see   like   to   the

We see Sam.

Sam is the cat.

Am I a cat?

Is Cam a cat?

We are the  .

We like Sam.

We go to see Sam!

 Draw what will happen next in the story.

Letters and Sounds

Phonics

 Trace and read the words. Draw a line from each word to its picture.

___ mat ___ ★

___ cat ___ ★

___ sat ___ ★

 ★

 ★

 ★

 Circle the words that rhyme with at.

(at)   cat   Tam   mat

Cam   Sam   am   sat

Words to Know

Read the words in the box. Then read the story.

Words to Know

a   are   go   I   like   is   see   the   to   we

We are at the 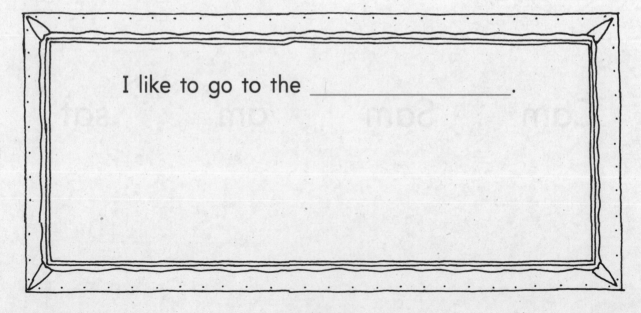 .

We see a cat.

The cat is a _____ .

I like the cat.

We like to go to the _____ .

✏️ Think about places that you like to visit. Write about and draw your ideas.

I like to go to the _____ .

Name _____

Words with Short *a*

What Is a Pal?
Phonics: Short *a*

 Write the missing letter. Read the word.

1.

___ a t

2.

___ a t

3.

D ___ n

4.

c ___ t

5.

___ a n

6.

S ___ m

Words to Know

✏️ Complete the sentences. Write a word from the box on each line.

Words to Know

with	help	and	you	play	be

1. Look at Cam _____ Sam.

2. What will this _____?

3. I like to _____ .

4. She can _____ .

5. Come _____ me, Sam!

6. _____ can go down.

Consonants *s, n, d*

Name each picture. Think of the beginning sound. Write **s**, **n**, or **d**.

1.

_____
- - - - -
_____

2.

_____
- - - - -
_____

3.

_____
- - - - -
_____

4.

_____
- - - - -
_____

5.

_____
- - - - -
_____

6.

_____
- - - - -
_____

Spelling Words with the Short *a* Sound

✏️ Sort the words. Write the correct Spelling Words in each column.

Words that have 2 letters	Words that have 3 letters
_____	_____
_____	_____
_____	_____
_____	_____
_____	_____

Spelling Words

am
at
sat
man
dad
mat

4

Nouns for People and Animals

✏️ Listen to the nouns in the Word Bank. Read along. Write nouns from the box to name the people and animals in the picture.

Word Bank

bird

fireman

grandma

dog

_____   _____

_____   _____

Giving Details

✏️ Listen to the words in the Word Bank. Read along. Add two details to this picture of two pals. Then write labels that tell who and what.

Word Bank

| cap | bat | bike | boy |
| Sam | Tom | pads | play |

Consonants *p, f*

 Name each picture. Think of the beginning sound. Write **p** or **f**.

1.

_____

2.

_____

3.

_____

4.

_____

5.

_____

6.

_____

7.

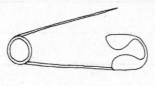

_____

8.

_____

9.

_____

Reader's Guide

What Is a Pal?

Letters to Pals

Be a pal. Write letters to your pals.

Read pages 16–17. Find ideas in the words and pictures about how pals can help. Write a letter to a pal. Ask for help with something.

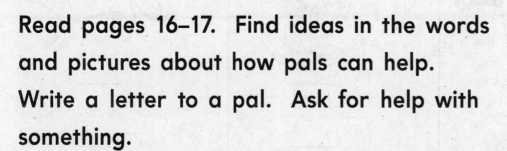

Dear _____ ,

_____

Please help me _____

_____

_____

_____

Your pal,

_____

_____

Name _____ Date _____

Read pages 22–25. Find ideas in the selection about what pals do. What will you do with a pal? Write a letter. Draw a picture.

_____

Dear _____,

_____

Will you _____ with me?

Your pal,

_____

Spelling Words with the Short *a* Sound

What Is a Pal?
Spelling: Words with Short *a*

✏️ Write the missing letter to complete each Spelling Word. Then write the word.

Spelling Words

am
at
sat
man
dad
mat

1. s ___ t _____

2. m ___ n _____

3. m ___ t _____

4. ___ t _____

5. d ___ d _____

6. ___ m _____

Words That Name Places or Things

✏️ Listen to the nouns in the Word Bank. Read along. Write a noun from the box to name each picture.

Word Bank

car

rope

park

plate

city

1. 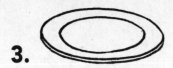 _____

2.  _____

3.  _____

4.  _____

5.  _____

My Pals

 Draw four pals. Show details that tell who, what, and where.

My Pals

 Write labels for your pictures.

Name _____

Spelling Words with the Short *a* Sound

✏️ **Write the correct word to complete each sentence.**

_____

- - - - - - - - - - - - - - - -

1. This _____ is for the cat. (mat, dad)

_____

- - - - - - - - - - - - - - - -

2. I _____ with it. (dad, sat)

_____

- - - - - - - - - - - - - - - -

3. I _____ mad. (mat, am)

_____

- - - - - - - - - - - - - - - -

4. Pat is _____ the play. (at, am)

_____

- - - - - - - - - - - - - - - -

5. We like the _____ . (man, at)

_____

- - - - - - - - - - - - - - - -

6. We sat on _____ . (at, dad)

Spiral Review

Circle the correct word in each box to name each person and pet.

1.

| sam |
| Sam |

| al |
| Al |

2.

| Sal |
| sal |

| Gam |
| gam |

3.

| dan |
| Dan |

| cal |
| Cal |

4.

| Cam |
| cam |

| Mag |
| mag |

Grammar in Writing

Words that name people, animals, places, and things are called **nouns**. Use nouns to name people, animals, places, and things when you write.

The <u>boy</u> smiles.

The <u>dog</u> runs.

The <u>stick</u> flies.

The <u>park</u> is fun.

✏️ **Listen to the nouns in the Word Bank, and to the sentences. Read along. Look at the picture. Write nouns from the box to finish the sentences.**

Word Bank

food

girl

cat

yard

_____

1. The _____ plays.

_____

2. The _____ cooks.

_____

3. The _____ is crowded.

_____

4. The _____ sleeps.

Words with Short *i*

 Write the missing letter. Read the word.

1.

s __ t

2.

T __ m

3.

p __ n

4.

f __ n

5.

s __ p

6.

h __ t

Words to Know

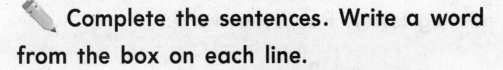 Complete the sentences. Write a word from the box on each line.

Words to Know

| he | look | have | too | for | what |

_____

- - - - - - - - - - - - - - -

1. I will _____ for the cat.

_____

- - - - - - - - - - - - - - -

2. _____ is a good cat.

_____

- - - - - - - - - - - - - - - - -

3. My dad will look, _____ .

_____

- - - - - - - - - - - - - - - - -

4. He will help me look _____ the cat.

_____

- - - - - - - - - - - - - -

5. _____ is this?

_____

- - - - - - - - - - - - - - -

6. I _____ the cat!

17

Consonants *r, h, /z/s*

 Write the missing letter. Read the word.

1.

__ a m

2.

h i __

3.

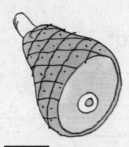

__ a m

4.

__ a n

5.

__ i p

6.

__ a t

Spelling Words with the Short *i* Sound

✏️ Sort the words. Write the correct Spelling Words in each column.

Words that have 2 letters	Words that have 3 letters

Spelling Words

if
is
him
rip
fit
pin

Name _____

Words That Show Ownership

Listen to the possessive nouns in the Word Bank. Read along. Write a possessive noun from the bank to name each picture.

Word Bank

boy's   man's   hen's   cat's

1. one _____ bag

2. a _____ dish

3. one _____ nest

4. a _____ glove

Details

🖊 Listen to the words in the Word Bank. Read along. Fill in each line to write captions for the picture. Choose words from the Word Bank or use your own.

Word Bank

vests
paddles
river
boat
flowers

_____

Mac is in the _____.

_____

Ma and Dad have _____.

_____

We will _____.

Consonants *b, g*

✏️ Name each picture. Think of the ending sound. Write **b** or **g**.

1.

_____
- - - - - - -
_____

2.

_____
- - - - - - -
_____

3.

_____
- - - - - - -
_____

4.

_____
- - - - - - -
_____

5.

_____
- - - - - - -
_____

6.

_____
- - - - - - -
_____

The Storm

A Dog's Story

My pal Rip spent time in a storm.

Read pages 48–49. Help Rip tell his pal Skip about the storm.

First, Tim and I went to _____.

_____

Next, we saw _____.

I felt _____.

Read pages 50–53. Tell how Pop helps Tim and Rip.

Pop gave Tim _____

_____

_____ .

Pop gave me _____ .

I felt _____ .

Then Pop sat and read. We _____

_____ .

Spelling Words with the Short *i* Sound

✏️ Write the missing letter to complete each Spelling Word. Then write the word.

if
is
him
rip
fit
pin

_____
- - - - -
1. f ____ t   _____

_____
- - - - -
2. p ____ n   _____

_____
- - - - -
3. r ____ p   _____

_____
- - - - -
4. ____ f   _____

_____
- - - - -
5. h ____ m   _____

_____
- - - - -
6. ____ s   _____

Words That Show Ownership

Listen to the possessive nouns in the Word Bank. Read along. Write a possessive noun from the bank to name each picture.

Word Bank

man's   cat's   bird's   girl's

1. a _____ tail

2. the _____ doll

3. a _____ glasses

4. the _____ nest

Planning My Caption

 Draw a picture of your family in a
favorite place.

My Family

[drawing box]

✏️ Write captions that tell about your picture.

_____

- - - - - - - - - - - - -

_____

- - - - - - - - - - - - -

_____

- - - - - - - - - - - - -

_____

Spelling Words with the Short *i* Sound

✏️ Write the correct word to complete each sentence.

_____

- - - - - - - - - - - - - - - - - - -

1. We play with _____ . (is, him)

_____

- - - - - - - - - - - - - - - - - - -

2. What did you _____ ? (rip, if)

_____

- - - - - - - - - - - - - - - - - - -

3. Kip _____ a pal. (is, him)

_____

- - - - - - - - - - - - - - - - - - -

4. Do you have a _____ ? (pin, him)

_____

- - - - - - - - - - - - - - - - - - -

5. Can the hat _____ ? (pin, fit)

_____

- - - - - - - - - - - - - - - - - - -

6. Will you play _____ I do? (fit, if)

Spiral Review

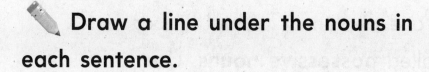 Draw a line under the nouns in each sentence.

1. The dog is under the bed.

2. Our house is near the school.

3. The girl and boy are reading.

4. One bird is in that tree.

5. That man lives in the city.

Grammar in Writing

Words that show that one person or animal has or owns something are called **possessive nouns**. Use possessive nouns to show ownership when you write.

The <u>man's</u> scarf is warm.

 Listen to the possessive nouns in the Word Bank. Read along. Write a possessive noun from the bank in the sentence about each picture.

Word Bank

cat's
boy's
girl's
dog's

1. The _____ bike is new.

2. The _____ hat is big

3. The _____ bed looks soft.

4. The _____ tail is long.

Words with Short *o*

 Name each picture. Color the pictures
with short o.

Words to Know

✏️ Complete the sentences. Write a word from the box on each line.

Words to Know

| do | find | funny | sing | no | they |

_____

_ _ _ _ _ _ _ _ _ _ _ _ _

1. Look at the _____ cat!

_____

_ _ _ _ _ _ _ _ _ _ _ _ _

2. _____ like to help.

_____

_ _ _ _ _ _ _ _ _ _ _ _ _

3. What will he _____ now?

_____

_ _ _ _ _ _ _ _ _ _ _ _ _

4. Dan will _____ now.

_____

_ _ _ _ _ _ _ _ _ _ _ _ _

5. _____, he did not see the cat.

_____

_ _ _ _ _ _ _ _ _ _ _ _ _

6. We can _____ a mat for you.

Consonants *l, x*

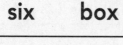 Finish the rhymes. Write one of the words from the box on the line.

six   box

Look at the fox.

___ ___ ___

- - - - - - - - - - - - -

It is on the ___ ___ ___ .

lot   log

Bob did not jog.

___ ___ ___

- - - - - - - - - - - - -

Bob sat on a ___ ___ ___ .

Spelling Words with the Short *o* Sound

✏️ Sort the words. Write the correct Spelling Words in each column.

Words that rhyme	Words that do not rhyme
_____	_____
_____	_____
_____	_____
_____	_____
_____	_____
_____	_____
_____	_____

Spelling Words

log
dot
top
hot
lot
ox

34

Name _____

Action Verbs

 Listen to the verbs in the Word Bank.
Read along. Write verbs from the box to tell
about the actions in the pictures.

Word Bank

eat

run

drink

draw

1. _____

- - - - - - - - - - - - - - - -

_____

2. _____

- - - - - - - - - - - - - - - -

_____

3. _____

- - - - - - - - - - - - - - - -

_____

4. _____

- - - - - - - - - - - - - - - -

_____

Using Exact Nouns

Draw two people at school. Show each one doing something different.

Listen to the words in the box. Read along. Write two sentences about your pictures. Tell what each person is doing.

Who	Action Verb	Exact Noun

Who	Action Verb	Exact Noun

ball	book	drum	fish	games
paper	piano	picture	song	teacher

Words with Inflection -s

✏️ Name each picture. Write the word. Use words in the box.

sits digs pats sips bats mops

1.

_____

- - - - - - - - - - - - - - -

2.

_____

- - - - - - - - - - - - - - -

3.

_____

- - - - - - - - - - - - - - -

4.

_____

- - - - - - - - - - - - - - -

5.

_____

- - - - - - - - - - - - - - -

6.

_____

- - - - - - - - - - - - - - -

Curious George Goes to School

A Day at School

Hi! I am in Mr. Apple's class. Today, a monkey came to my school!

Read pages 72–74. Write what happened at school.

Curious George came to school. I had fun with George

when we _____.

_____ .

_____ .

_____ .

Read pages 75–81.

George made a big mess. It looked _____

_____

- - - - - - - - - - - - - - - - - - - -

_____ .

George needed help. I helped by _____

_____

- - - - - - - - - - - - - - - - - - - -

_____ .

I want George to come back because _____

_____

- - - - - - - - - - - - - - - - - - - -

_____

_____

- - - - - - - - - - - - - - - - - - - -

_____

Spelling Words with the Short *o* Sound

✏️ Write the missing letter to complete each Spelling Word. Then write the word.

log
dot
hot
top
lot
ox

1. l ___ t _____

2. l ___ g _____

3. h ___ t _____

4. ___ x _____

5. t ___ p _____

6. d ___ t _____

Name _____

More Words That Show Action

✏️ Listen to the verbs in the Word Bank. Read along. Write a verb from the box to name each action in the picture.

Word Bank

climb
slide
jump
swing
throw

_____   _____

- - - - - - - - - - - - -   - - - - - - - - - - - - -

_____   _____

_____   _____

- - - - - - - - - - - - -   - - - - - - - - - - - - -

_____   _____

_____

- - - - - - - - - - - - -

Planning My Sentences

Write an action verb at the top of each box. Draw a picture to go with the verb.

Name _____

Spelling Words with the Short *o* Sound

✏️ Write the correct word to complete each sentence.

_____

- - - - - - - - - - - - - - - - -

1. A _____ is not big.   (hot, dot)

_____

- - - - - - - - - - - - - - - - -

2. The _____ is big.   (log, hot)

_____

- - - - - - - - - - - - - - - - -

3. We have a _____ of cats.   (lot, top)

_____

- - - - - - - - - - - - - - - - -

4. Pam is at the _____ .   (dog, top)

_____

- - - - - - - - - - - - - - - - -

5. Do you have a _____ pot?   (hot, log)

_____

- - - - - - - - - - - - - - - - -

6. Did you ever see an _____ ?   (ox, hot)

Name _____

Lesson 3
READER'S NOTEBOOK

Curious George
at School
Grammar

Spiral Review

✏️ Circle the possessive noun that shows ownership. Then write the possessive noun.

1. A boy's bike is in the yard.

_____
- - - - - - - - - - - - - - - - - - - -
_____

2. The cat's food is in the dish.

_____
- - - - - - - - - - - - - - - - - - - -
_____

3. The man's car is red.

_____
- - - - - - - - - - - - - - - - - - - -
_____

4. That ball is the dog's toy.

_____
- - - - - - - - - - - - - - - - - - - -
_____

5. A girl's map is over there.

_____
- - - - - - - - - - - - - - - - - - - -
_____

Grammar in Writing

Words that tell what people and animals
do are called **verbs**.

They <u>run</u> on the playground.

✏️ **Circle the verb to finish each sentence.
Write the verb on the line.**

_____
- - - - - - - - - - - - - - - - -

1. Sal can _____ with a bat.

   hit   fit

   _____
   - - - - - - - - - - - - - -

2. They _____ big bags.

   make   sit

   _____
   - - - - - - - - - - - - -

3. We _____ the dogs.

   go   see

   _____
   - - - - - - - - - - - - -

4. Bob and Meg _____ a cat.

   find   hop

Words with Short *e*

✏️ Circle the word that matches each picture.

1.

win   web

2.

mat   men

3.

net   can

4.

pen   pin

5.

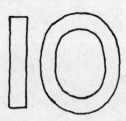

ten   tin

6.

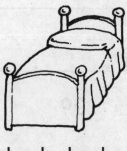

bad   bed

Name _____

Words to Know

✏️ Complete the sentences. Write a word from the box on each line.

Words to Know

| all | does | here | me | my | who |

_____

- - - - - - - - - - - - - - - - - -

1. Lin is _____ pal.

_____

- - - - - - - - - - - - - - - - - -

2. Sam will come _____ to play.

_____

- - - - - - - - - - - - - - - - - -

3. He likes to play with _____ .

_____

- - - - - - - - - - - - - - - - - -

4. I will see _____ is there.

_____

- - - - - - - - - - - - - - - - - -

5. Sam _____ a funny trick.

_____

- - - - - - - - - - - - - - - - - -

6. We will take up _____ the mats.

Name _____

Consonants *y, w*

✏️ Name each picture. Think of the
beginning sound. Write **y** or **w**.

1.

_____
- - - - -
_____

2.

_____
- - - - -
_____

3.

_____
- - - - -
_____

4.

_____
- - - - -
_____

5.

_____
- - - - -
_____

6.

_____
- - - - -
_____

Spelling Words with the Short *e* Sound

✏️ **Sort the words. Write the correct Spelling Words in each column.**

Words that rhyme with **get**	Words that rhyme with **den**	Words that do not rhyme
_____	_____	_____
_____	_____	_____
_____	_____	_____
_____	_____	_____

Spelling Words

yet

web

pen

wet

leg

hen

Adjectives for Size

✏️ Listen to the adjectives. Read along. Circle the adjective that describes what the picture shows. Write the adjective.

1.

small _____

big _____

2.

long _____

short _____

3.

narrow _____

wide _____

4.

short _____

tall _____

Using Words That Are Just Right

🖉 Cross out the word that is the same in each sentence. Listen to the words in the box. Read along. Write a better word from the box.

> ### Word Bank
>
> busy   large   new   sweet
> round   kind   square   tall

1. Our town has a good market. _____

2. Mom and I get good apples there. _____

3. We got a good cake for Dad. _____

4. The man that helps us is good. _____

Consonants *k, v, j*

✏️ Name each picture. Think of the
beginning sound. Write **k, v,** or **j**.

1.

_____

- - - - - - -

2.

_____

- - - - - - -

3.

_____

- - - - - - -

4.

_____

- - - - - - -

5.

_____

- - - - - - -

6.

_____

- - - - - - -

7.

_____

- - - - - - -

8.

_____

- - - - - - -

9.

_____

- - - - - - -

Lucia's Neighborhood

Lucia's Map

Lucia's uncle is coming to visit! Draw a map to help him find her.

Read pages 100–105 again. Draw where each place is. Write the place name.

Read pages 106–109. Make another map for this part of the story. Draw where each place is. Write the place name.

Spelling Words with the Short *e* Sound

Write the missing letter to complete each Spelling Word. Then write the word.

____
1. y ___ t
____

_ _ _ _
2. h ___ n
____

_ _ _ _
3. w ___ b
____

_ _ _ _
4. l ___ g
____

_ _ _ _
5. p ___ n
____

_ _ _ _
6. w ___ t

_____
_____
_____
_____
_____
_____
_____
_____
_____
_____
_____
_____

Adjectives for Shape

 Listen to and follow the directions.

1. Circle the shape that is **round**.

2. Circle the shape that is **flat**.

3. Circle the shape that is **square**.

4. Circle the shape that is **curved**.

Spelling Words with the Short *e* Sound

✏️ **Write the correct word to complete each sentence.**

_____
- - - - - - - - - - - - - - - -

1. He is not here _____ .   (yet, web)

_____
- - - - - - - - - - - - - - - -

2. The _____ is big.   (wet, hen)

_____
- - - - - - - - - - - - - - - -

3. My _____ is red.   (pen, wet)

_____
- - - - - - - - - - - - - - - -

4. The dog is all _____ .   (wet, hen)

_____
- - - - - - - - - - - - - - - -

5. I can hop on my _____ .   (yet, leg)

_____
- - - - - - - - - - - - - - - -

6. I can see a _____ .   (wet, web)

Name _____

Spiral Review

 Listen to the verbs in the Word Bank. Read along. Write verbs from the bank to tell about the actions in the pictures.

Word Bank

hop
dig
read
swim

1. _____

   - - - - - - - - - -

   _____

2. _____

   - - - - - - - - - -

   _____

3. _____

   - - - - - - - - - -

   _____

4. _____

   - - - - - - - - - -

   _____

Grammar in Writing

Words that describe people, animals, or things are called **adjectives**. Adjectives can describe size or shape.

> The house is <u>big</u>. (size)
> The truck is <u>wide</u>. (shape)

✏️ **Listen to the adjectives in the Word Banks. Read along. Write on the line an adjective for size.**

Word Bank

long
little

_____

1. A leg is _____ .

2. A dot is _____ .

✏️ **Write on the line an adjective for shape.**

Word Bank

flat
round

_____

3. A map is _____ .

4. A log is _____ .

Words with Short *u*

 Write the missing letter. Read the word.

1.

p __ p

2.

c __ p

3.

m __ d

4.

t __ b

5.

f __ n

6.

__ p

Words to Know

Draw a line to the word that completes the sentence. Write the word on the line.

_____

1. Tom will _____ the sled.   **hold**

2. It was _____ to sit for a bit.   **full**

3. All the bags are _____ .   **pull**

4. Mel has _____ pals.   **friend**

5. Cam is my _____ .   **good**

6. Mom will _____ my books for me.   **many**

More Words with Short *u*

 Write the missing letter. Read the word.

1.

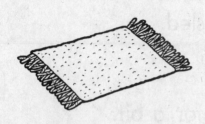

___ u g

2.

___ u n

3.

___ u s

4.

___ u t

5.

___ u g

6.

___ u n

Spelling Words with the Short *u* Sound

✏️ Sort the words. Write the correct Spelling Words in each column.

Spelling Words

up
bug
mud
nut
hug
tub

Words that rhyme	Words that do not rhyme
_____	_____
_____	_____
_____	_____
_____	_____
_____	_____
_____	_____
_____	_____

Adjectives for Color

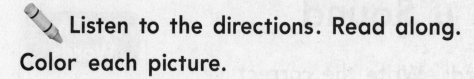 Listen to the directions. Read along.
Color each picture.

1. Color the cap **blue**.

2. Color the toy **yellow**.

3. Color the ball **orange**.

4. Color the apple **red**.

5. Color the bug **black**.

Telling More

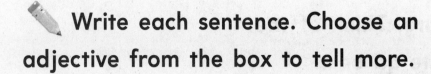 **Write each sentence. Choose an adjective from the box to tell more.**

big	many	ten	mad
bad	good	red	tan
sad	funny	hot	wet

1. Dad and I get on a bus.

_____

- - - - - - - - - - - - - - - -

Dad and I get on a _____ bus.

2. We go to a park.

_____

- - - - - - - - - - - - - - - -

We go to a _____ park.

3. We see a man with pets.

_____

- - - - - - - - - - - - - - - -

We see a man with _____ pets.

4. Dad gets me a hat!

_____

- - - - - - - - - - - - - - - -

Dad gets me a _____ hat!

Consonants *qu*, *z*

✏️ Name each picture. Think of the beginning sound. Write **qu** or **z**.

1.

_____
- - - - - - -
_____

2.

_____
- - - - - - -
_____

3.

_____
- - - - - - -
_____

4.
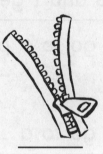

_____
- - - - - - -
_____

5.

_____
- - - - - - -
_____

6.

_____
- - - - - - -
_____

Gus Takes the Train

Gus's Trip

Read pages 128–132. Gus needs a ticket to get on the train. A ticket tells the conductor many things.

Draw a ticket for Gus. Write his name, where he is going, and what he is bringing with him.

Read pages 133–137. Gus meets a friend.
Gus draws and writes in his journal. Draw
the two friends on the train. Write about
what they do.

 Gus's Journal

Friends

_____

- -

_____

- -

_____

Spelling Words with the Short *u* Sound

Write the missing letter to complete each Spelling Word. Then write the word.

Spelling Words

up
bug
mud
nut
hug
tub

1. n ___ t

   _____

2. b ___ g

   _____

3. m ___ d

   _____

4. ___ p

   _____

5. t ___ b

   _____

6. h ___ g

   _____

69

Adjectives for Number

✏️ Listen to the adjectives in the Word Bank. Read along. Write a word from the box to describe each picture.

Word Bank

two three four six

1.

_____

- - - - - - - - - - - - - -

_____

2.

_____

- - - - - - - - - - - - - -

_____

3.

_____

- - - - - - - - - - - - - -

_____

4.

_____

- - - - - - - - - - - - - -

_____

70

Spelling Words with the Short *u* Sound

Write the correct word to complete each sentence.

_____

1. Dad likes to _____ the cat.   (up, hug)

_____

2. A _____ is on my leg!   (bug, hug)

_____

3. Put the mat _____ on top.   (nut, up)

_____

4. I got wet in the _____.   (tub, bug)

_____

5. Do you have a _____ for me?   (nut, mud)

_____

6. The pig likes to play in the _____.
(mud, hug)

Spiral Review

✏️ Listen to the adjectives in the Word Bank. Read along. Write an adjective from the Bank to tell about each picture.

1. The hoop is _____.

2. The ant is _____.

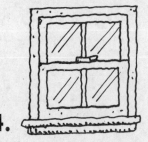

3. The rope is _____.

4. The window is _____.

Grammar in Writing

Words that describe people, places, animals, or things are called **adjectives**. Adjectives can describe color and number.

The train is <u>black</u>. The <u>five</u> seats are <u>red</u>.

Finish each sentence with an adjective for number. Use the Word Bank.

Word Bank

one

three

_____

- - - - - - - - - - - - - - -

1. I see _____ flowers.

_____

- - - - - - - - - - - - - - -

2. I see _____ cat.

Listen to and follow the directions.

3. Draw **two** apples.

Color the apples **red**.

4. Draw **four** bugs.

Color the bugs **black**.

Double Final Consonants and *ck*

Jack and the Wolf
Phonics: Double Final
Consonants and *ck*

✏ Name each picture. Write the letters from the box that stand for the ending sound.

ck	gg	ss	ll

1.

q u a ___ ___

2.

h i ___ ___

3.

l o ___ ___

4.

e ___ ___

5.

d o ___ ___

6.

s o ___ ___

74

Name _____

Words to Know

 Fill in the blanks to complete the sentences.
Write a word from the box on each line.

Words to Know

hear	call	come
said	every	away

_____

1. Does _____ dog like to play?

_____

2. Mem _____ she did not see the dog.

_____

3. Jack will _____ to help me.

_____

4. Sam and Jill are far _____ .

_____

5. Did you _____ the clock tick?

_____

6. Von will _____ on me to sing.

Double Final Consonants and *ck*

✏️ Circle the letters to make the word that matches the picture. Write the letters.

1.

b u _ _ _ _ _ _
ck   zz

2.

t a _ _ _ _ _ _
ss   ck

3.

p u _ _ _ _ _ _
gg   ff

4.

m i _ _ _ _ _ _
ss   tt

5.

h i _ _ _ _ _ _
ss   ll

6.

d u _ _ _ _ _ _
ll   ck

Name _____

Spelling Words with the Short *a* Sound

Jack and the Wolf
Spelling: Words with
Short *a*

✏️ Sort the words. Write the correct Spelling Words in each column.

Spelling Words

an
bad
can
had
cat
ran

Words that begin with a vowel	Words that begin with a consonant
_____	_____
- - - - - - - - - -	- - - - - - - - - -
_____	_____
- - - - - - - - - -	- - - - - - - - - -
_____	_____
- - - - - - - - - -	- - - - - - - - - -
_____	_____
- - - - - - - - - -	- - - - - - - - - -
_____	_____
- - - - - - - - - -	- - - - - - - - - -
_____	_____

What Is a Sentence?

 Draw a line under each sentence.

1. The friends play.

2. a cat

3. The dog runs.

4. sit

 Draw lines to make sentences.

5. The hen   sits on a rock.

6. Gram   like to sing.

7. Jack   sits on eggs.

8. We   makes a doll.

Using Sense Words

deep
hot
loud
small
soft
sunny
sweet
warm

🖊 Listen to the sense words in the box and the sentences below. Read along. Write words from the box to finish the sentences about the picture.

_____

1. The bananas smell _____ .

_____

2. The lion's fur feels _____ .

_____

3. The seal's bark sounds _____ .

_____

4. The monkeys look _____

Short *a*, Double Final Consonants, and *ck*

✏️ Name each picture. Write words from the box.

fill	wag	yam	quick	van	neck

1.

_____

- - - - - - - - - - - - - - - -

_____

2.

_____

- - - - - - - - - - - - - - - -

_____

3.

_____

- - - - - - - - - - - - - - - -

_____

4.

_____

- - - - - - - - - - - - - - - -

_____

5.

_____

- - - - - - - - - - - - - - - -

_____

6.

_____

- - - - - - - - - - - - - - - -

_____

Reader's Guide

Jack and the Wolf

Jack's Rules

Jack has a job. He takes care of the sheep.

Read pages 16–17. What does Jack do?

What rules is he following?

Rules for Jack

1. _____.

2. _____.

3. _____.

Name _____ Date _____

**Read pages 18–29. Jack learns
a lesson. Write more rules Jack will
follow to do his job better.**

4. _____
_____
_____ .

5. _____
_____
_____ .

6. _____
_____
_____ .

Spelling Words with the Short *a* Sound

Spelling Words
an
bad
can
had
cat
ran

🖉 Write the Spelling Words that rhyme with **man**.

_____

1. _____

_____

2. _____

_____

3. _____

🖉 Write the Spelling Words that rhyme with **dad**.

_____   _____

4. _____   5. _____

🖉 Write the Spelling Word that rhymes with **sat**.

_____

6. _____

Is It a Sentence?

 Draw a line under each sentence.

1. The dog naps.

naps

2. Tim and Jim

Tim and Jim run away.

3. the friends

The friends come to help.

4. The man sits down.

sits

5. sings

He sings.

6. get up

The dog will get up.

Planning My Sentences

✏️ Listen to the labels in the web and read along. Write and draw details that describe your topic. You do not have to write words for every sense.

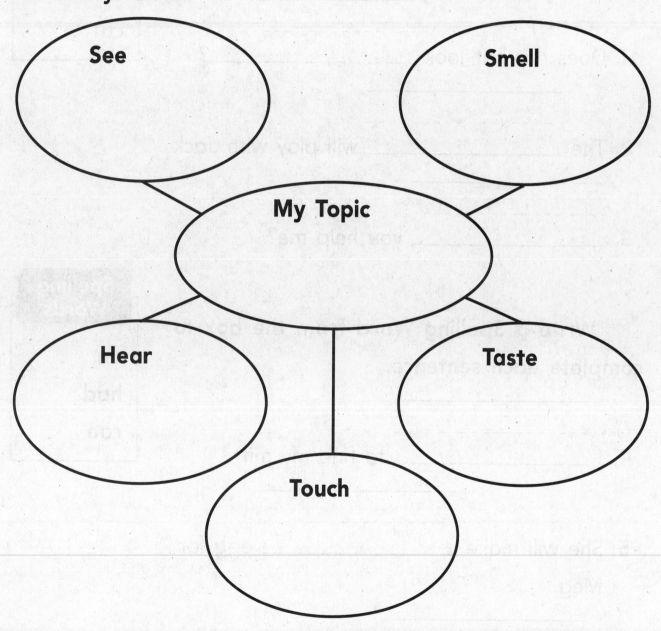

Spelling Words with the Short *a* Sound

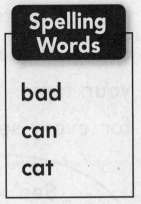

Spelling Words

bad

can

cat

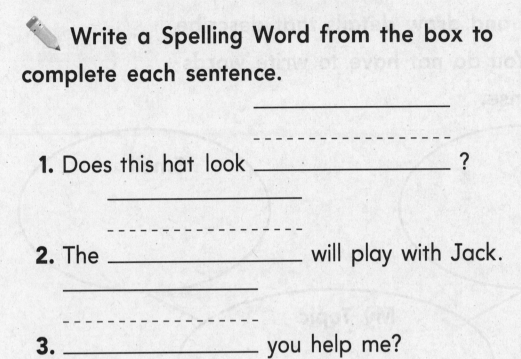 Write a Spelling Word from the box to complete each sentence.

_____

- - - - - - - - - - - - - - - -

1. Does this hat look _____ ?

_____

- - - - - - - - - - - - - -

2. The _____ will play with Jack.

_____

- - - - - - - - - - - - - - -

3. _____ you help me?

Spelling Words

an

had

ran

Write a Spelling Word from the box to complete each sentence.

_____

- - - - - - - - - - - - -

4. I _____ to find my mitt.

_____

- - - - - - - - - - - - - -

5. She will make _____ egg for Meg.

_____

- - - - - - - - - - - -

6. I _____ out to play.

Name _____

Spiral Review

 Listen to the adjectives in the Word
Bank. Read along. Write a word from
the bank to tell about each picture.

Word Bank

three

six

four

1. I see _____ balls.

2. I see _____ birds.

3. I see _____ pears.

 Listen to and follow the directions.

4. Draw two bananas.
   Color the bananas yellow.

5. Draw five nuts.
   Color the nuts brown.

Grammar in Writing

A **sentence** is a group of words. A sentence tells who or what. It also tells what someone or something does or did.

Sentence	Not a Sentence
All the ducks sit.	sit
	all the ducks

Circle the two groups of words that are not sentences.

1. We have fun.   **3.** The dog runs away.

2. get mad   **4.** Jack

Add words to make the word groups you circled complete sentences. Write the new sentences.

_____

5. _____

_____

6. _____

Blends with *r*

 Name each picture. Write letters from
the box to complete the word.

br	cr	dr	gr	tr

1.

__ __ i n

2.

__ __ i m

3.

__ __ i p

4.

__ __ i b

5.

__ __ i p

6.

__ __ i m

Name _____

Lesson 7
READER'S NOTEBOOK

How Animals
Communicate
High-Frequency Words

Words to Know

 Fill in the blanks to complete the sentences.

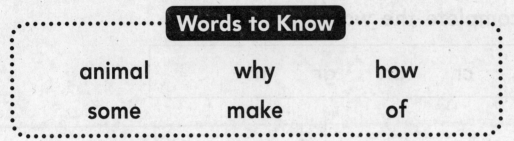

Words to Know

animal	why	how
some	make	of

_____

1. Tell me _____ you like to sing.

_____

2. The bug can _____ a hut out of mud!

_____

3. Bob will go with _____ friends.

_____

4. He can tell you _____ to bat.

_____

5. Six _____ the bags are full.

_____

6. What _____ do you have as a pet?

Blends with *r*

Name each picture. Circle the letters that stand for the beginning sounds. Write the letters to make the word.

1.

fr   cr

___ ___

___ ___ a b

2.

pr   tr

___ ___

___ ___ a p

3.

pr   fr

___ ___

___ ___ o g

4.

gr   pr

___ ___

___ ___ i l l

5.

dr   gr

___ ___

___ ___ u m

6.

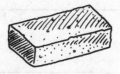

gr   br

___ ___

___ ___ i c k

Name _____

Spelling Words with the Short *i* Sound

✏️ Sort the words. Write the correct Spelling Words in each column.

Words that begin with a vowel	Words that begin with a consonant
_____	_____
------------------	------------------
_____	_____
------------------	------------------
_____	_____
------------------	------------------
_____	_____
------------------	------------------

Spelling Words

in

will

did

sit

six

big

Commas in a Series

✏ Listen to each sentence. Read along.
Add commas where they belong.

1. They had dogs hens   chicks.

2. Cats dogs   fish are pets.

3. My dog can sit beg   run.

4. I saw frogs bugs   fish.

5. A bull kicks jumps   runs.

Name _____

Adjectives

✏️ Draw a picture of an animal doing something.

Word Bank

big

small

slow

loud

quiet

soft

young

✏️ Listen to the adjectives in the Word Bank. Read along. Complete each sentence with a word from the Word Bank or your own adjective.

_____
- - - - - - - - - - - - - - - - - - -

1. The animal is _____ .

_____
- - - - - - - - - - - - - - - - - - -

2. The animal is _____ .

_____
- - - - - - - - - - - - - - - - - - -

3. The animal is _____ .

_____
- - - - - - - - - - - - - - - - - - -

4. The animal is _____ .

Short *i* and Blends with *r*

Write words that rhyme. Use the words in the box.

trick grab dress drill grass quit tracks truck

1. brick

2. grill

3. press

4. crab

5. cracks

6. duck

7. sit

8. brass

Name _____ Date _____

Lesson 7
READER'S NOTEBOOK

How Animals
Communicate
Independent Reading

 **Reader's Guide**

How Animals Communicate

Make a Chart

You read about animal senses. Make a chart to show what you know.

Read pages 48–53. Fill in the chart.

This is a _____ .	I hear a _____ .
This is a _____ .	I hear a _____ .

What communication do you hear right now?

_____

_____

_____

Read pages 54–61. Fill in the chart.

This is a _____ _____ .	I see the dog _____ .
This is a _____ _____ .	I see the bee _____ .

How are you using your eyes to communicate right now?

_____
_____
_____
_____
_____

Spelling Words with the Short *i* Sound

 Circle the Spelling Word that names the picture. Then write the word.

Spelling Words

in
will
did
sit
six
big

1. six
sip

_____

- - - - - - - - - -

_____

2. pin
in

_____

- - - - - - - - - -

_____

3. fit
sit

_____

- - - - - - - - - -

_____

4. big
bag

_____

- - - - - - - - - -

_____

 Write a Spelling Word that rhymes with each word below.

_____

- - - - - - - - - -

5. hid
_____

_____

- - - - - - - - - -

6. fill
_____

Commas in a Series

Read each list of words. Write a sentence that uses the words in a list. Use commas and the word <u>and</u> where they belong.

sit	run	beg

_____

1. My dog can _____.

sing	read	draw

_____

2. I like to _____.

hop	swim	eat

_____

3. A frog can _____.

run	play	nap

_____

4. A cat can _____.

Planning My Poem

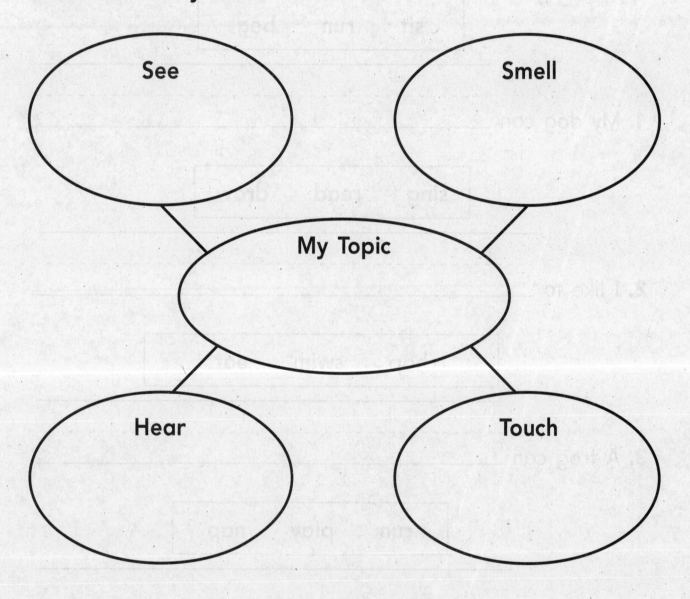 Write and draw details that describe your topic. Listen to the names of the senses and read along. You do not have to write words for every sense.

Spelling Words with the Short *i* Sound

✏️ Write the correct word to complete each sentence.

_____

- - - - - - - - - - - - - -

1. I have a _____ dog. (big, bag)

_____

- - - - - - - - - - - - - -

2. _____ you see my mat? (Dad, Did)

_____

- - - - - - - - - - - - - -

3. Jon will _____ down. (sit, sat)

_____

- - - - - - - - - - - - - -

4. _____ you help me with the cats? (Wall, Will)

_____

- - - - - - - - - - - - - -

5. I put the hat _____ my bag. (in, an)

_____

- - - - - - - - - - - - - -

6. The hen has _____ eggs. (mix, six)

Name _____

Spiral Review

✏️ Listen to the nouns in the Word Bank.
Read along. Write a noun from the box to
name each picture.

Word Bank

girl
pond
cat
bowl

1.  _____

2. 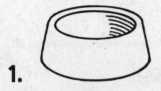 _____

3.  _____

4.  _____

102

Grammar in Writing

A sentence with a list of three items will have a comma after each of the first two items. The word *and* is used before the last item.

Example: I like red, blue, and green.

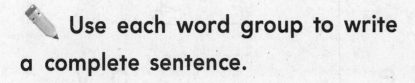 Use each word group to write a complete sentence.

1. bread   butter   jam

   _____

   - - - - - - - - - - - - - - - - -

   _____.

2. walk   run   hop

   _____

   - - - - - - - - - - - - - - - - -

   _____.

3. cats   dogs   fish

   _____

   - - - - - - - - - - - - - - - - -

   _____.

Blends with *l*

✏️ Name each picture. Write the first two letters to make the word.

1.

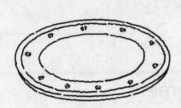

____ ____ ____

‐ ‐ ‐ ‐ ‐

____ ____ **a t e**

2.

____ ____ ____

‐ ‐ ‐ ‐ ‐

____ ____ **a y**

3.

____ ____ ____

____ ____ **o c k**

4.

‐ ‐ ‐ ‐ ‐

____ ____ **a d**

5.

____ ____ ____

‐ ‐ ‐ ‐ ‐

____ ____ **a t**

6.

____ ____ ____

‐ ‐ ‐ ‐ ‐

____ ____ **e d**

Words to Know

Choose the word that fits best in the sentence. Write the word on the line.

1. Jen will fix (her, she, today) bed.

_____

2. I (our, here, would) like to help.

_____

3. (Her, Now, She) is my friend.

_____

4. We have a lot to do (our, today, she).

_____

5. We did (she, here, our) job!

_____

6. We can play (our, now, her).

_____

Blends with *l*

 Circle the word to finish the sentence.
Write the word.

1.

_____

- - - - - - - - - - -

She will _____ .

slip   slap

2.

- - - - - - - - - - -

This is a _____ .

clam   blot

3.

_____

- - - - - - - - - - -

Who will _____ this?

slip   flip

4.

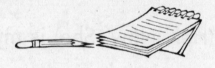

_____

- - - - - - - - - - -

I have a _____ .

plan   blab

5.

_____

- - - - - - - - -

This is a big _____ .

blot   flap

6.

_____

He is _____ to play.

clap   glad

Name _____

Spelling Words with the Short *o* Sound

Spelling Words

on
fox
got
hop
pop
not

✏️ Write the Spelling Words that rhyme with **dot.**

_____   _____

1. _____   2. _____

✏️ Write the Spelling Words that rhyme with **top.**

_____   _____

3. _____   4. _____

✏️ Write the Spelling Word that rhymes with **ox.**

_____

5. _____

✏️ Write the Spelling Word that rhymes with **Don.**

_____

6. _____

What Is a Statement?

 Draw a line under each statement.

1. He makes a drum.

2. sings

3. She plays well.

4. Our band will win.

5. Bill and Sam

6. Nick claps for us.

 Use a word from the box to make each group of words a statement.

Word Bank

listen

Meg

_____

7. _____ plays the drums.

8. Ken and Kim _____ .

Using Exact Adjectives

✏️ Fill in the blanks in the draft of the thank-you note. Listen to the adjectives in the Word Bank. Read along. Choose adjectives from the box. Write your own words, too.

Word Bank

hot	huge	icy	tall	round
soft	striped	sweet	green	yellow

_____

Dear _____,

Thank you for the _____

_____ . It is _____

_____ . I like the

_____ .

Blends with *l*

✏️ Name each picture. Circle the letters that stand for the beginning sounds. Write the word.

1.

cr   gr

_____

- - - - - - - - - -

_____

2.

fl   fr

_____

- - - - - - - - - -

_____

3.

fl   sl

_____

- - - - - - - - - -

_____

4.

br   dr

_____

- - - - - - - - - -

_____

5.

gr   dr

_____

- - - - - - - - - -

_____

6.

pl   bl

_____

- - - - - - - - - -

_____

Name _____ Date _____

 Reader's Guide

A Musical Day

How to Make a Band

Aunt Viv came over! We made a band.
Here are the steps.

Read pages 85–91. Look at the pictures.
Write how the girls make guitars.

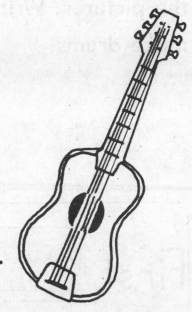

First, _____
_____
_____
_____ .

↓

Next, _____
_____ .

↓

Last, _____
_____ .

Read pages 89–93 again. Look at the pictures. Write how the boys make drums.

First, _____
_____
_____ .

↓

Next, _____
_____
_____ .

↓

Last, _____
_____ .

Name _____

Spelling Words with the Short *o* Sound

 Write the missing letter to complete each Spelling Word. Then write the word.

Spelling Words
on
got
fox
hop
pop
not

____

1. f ___ x   _____

____

2. n ___ t   _____

____

3. p ___ p   _____

____

4. h ___ p   _____

____

5. ___ n   _____

____

6. g ___ t   _____

Writing Statements

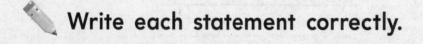 Circle the capital letter that begins each statement and the period that ends it.

1. Clem likes my song.

2. She sings for her mom.

3. Her mom sings, too.

4. They like to sing.

✏️ Write each statement correctly.

5. tess has a drum set

_____

- -

_____

6. she plays it a lot

_____

- -

_____

Planning My Thank-You Note

I will write my thank-you note to

_____

- -

_____ .

✏️ Draw a picture of what you are thankful for. Write some details for your note.

	I am thankful for	
_____		_____
- - - - - - - - -		- - - - - - - - -
_____		_____
- - - - - - - - -		- - - - - - - - -
_____		_____
- - - - - - - - -		- - - - - - - - -
_____		_____

Spelling Words with the Short *o* Sound

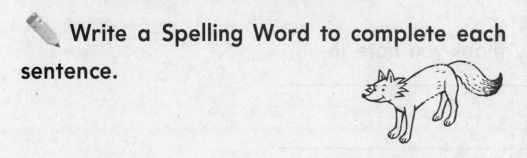 Write a Spelling Word to complete each sentence.

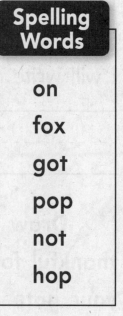

Spelling Words

on

fox

got

pop

not

hop

1. This animal is a _____ .

2. I _____ a dog from Bob.

3. I like caps but _____ hats.

4. The bag will _____ if you fill it up.

5. The fox will _____ off the box.

6. Do not sit _____ the bed.

Spiral Review

✏️ Listen to the verbs in the Word Bank. Read along. Write a verb from the box to name each action.

Word Bank

play

dance

sing

watch

1. _____

_ _ _ _ _ _ _ _ _ _ _ _ _ _ _

_____

2. _____

_ _ _ _ _ _ _ _ _ _ _ _ _ _ _

_____

3. _____

_ _ _ _ _ _ _ _ _ _ _ _ _ _ _

_____

4. _____

_ _ _ _ _ _ _ _ _ _ _ _ _ _ _

_____

Grammar in Writing

A statement begins with a **capital letter** and ends with a **period**.

✏️ Fix the mistakes in these statements. Use proofreading marks.

Example: we play the bells
≡   ∧

1. she hits a big drum

2. he holds a doll

3. they have big hats

4. we tap and sing

Proofreading Marks	
∧	add
≡	capital letter

118

Blends with *s*

✏️ Name each picture. Write the first two or three letters that stand for the beginning sounds. Use the letters from the box.

st	sw	sn	sk	str

1. _____

2. _____

3. _____

4. _____

5. _____

Words to Know

✏️ Circle the word that fits in each sentence. Write that word on the line.

This is my cat.

1. I like to (read, after, was).

_____

2. The cat (after, was, draw) in his bed.

_____

3. I like to (after, was, draw) animals.

_____

4. Here are (writes, pictures, reads) of my cat.

_____

5. Now I will (was, after, write) to my dad.

_____

6. I will help you (after, draw, read) I call Brad.

_____

Name _____

Blends with *s*

✏️ **Circle the word that finishes the sentence.**

Write the word.

1.

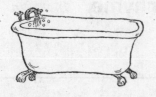

_____

Ann can _____ well.

spell   swim

2.

_____

Who made this _____?

spill   snag

3.

_____

I _____ in the tub.

sniff   scrub

4.

_____

This cat is not _____!

small   scrap

5.

_____

Pam likes to _____.

strum   smell

6.

_____

Kim will get a _____.

spin   snack

Name _____

Spelling Words with the Short *e* Sound

 Circle the word that names the picture. Then write the word.

1. bad
bed

_____

2. ten
tan

_____

Spelling Words
yes
let
red
ten
bed
get

 Write the Spelling Words that rhyme with **wet**.

3. _____

4. _____

Proofread each sentence. Circle the Spelling Word that is wrong. Write it correctly.

_____

5. I have a rud pen.

_____

6. I said yez.

_____

One and
More Than One

✏️ **Listen to the nouns and read along.**
Circle the noun for each picture below. Then
write the nouns you circled.

1. 　　bird　　birds　　--------------------

2. 　　boy　　boys　　--------------------

3. 　　ball　　balls　　--------------------

4. 　　tree　　trees　　--------------------

5. 　　cake　　cakes　　--------------------

Telling How Things Look

 Draw a picture of an animal.

one

two

three

four

blue

red

yellow

big

small

round

Finish the sentences that describe your animal. Listen to the words in the box. You can use these and other words you choose.

_____   _____

1. The _____ looks _____ .

2. Its _____ are _____ .

3. It has _____ .

Short *e* and Blends with *s*

✏️ Name each picture. Circle the letters that stand for the beginning sounds. Write the letters. Write the word.

1.  st
sw   ___ ___ ___ i m   _____

2.  ru
re   ___ ___ ___ s t   _____

3. 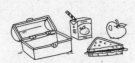 st
sn   ___ ___ ___ a c k   _____

4.  ve
ne   ___ ___ ___ s t   _____

5.  fl
sl   ___ ___ ___ i p   _____

6. 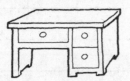 de
di   ___ ___ ___ s k   _____

 Reader's Guide

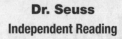

Dr. Seuss

A Funny Man

Read pages 112–115. Write what is funny about the picture on page 115.

_____

- -

_____
_____

- -

_____
_____

- -

_____ .

Read pages 116–118. Why is the Cat in the Hat in a few of the photos?

_____

- -

_____
_____

- -

_____
_____

- -

_____ .

Name _____ Date _____

Read pages 119–125. Now it's your turn to be funny! Ted wrote rhymes, and you can too. Write three words that rhyme. Write a funny sentence with your words.

_____

- -

_____

- -

_____ .

Spelling Words with the Short *e* Sound

Dr. Seuss
Spelling: Words with Short *e*

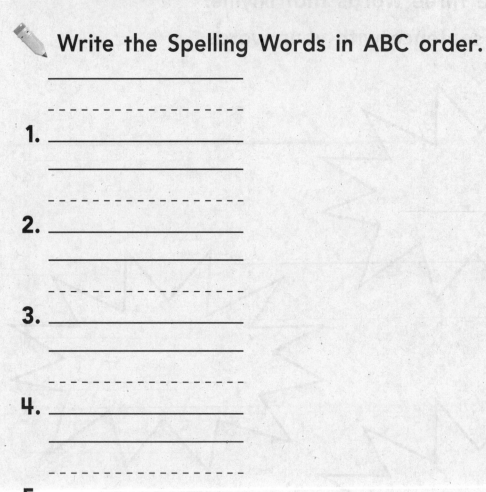 Write the Spelling Words in ABC order.

1. _____

2. _____

3. _____

4. _____

5. _____

6. _____

Spelling Words

yes

let

red

ten

bed

get

Special Plural Nouns

Listen to the nouns and read along.
Circle the noun for each picture below. Then
write the nouns you circled. Complete the
sentences with the correct verb.

1.   woman   women   ----------------

2.    man   men   ----------------

3.   man   men   ----------------

4.   child   children   ----------------

5. The women _____ . (sing, sings)

6. The child _____ . (walk, walks)

Spelling Words with the Short *e* Sound

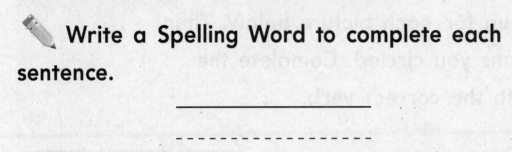 Write a Spelling Word to complete each sentence.

Spelling Words

yes

let

red

ten

bed

get

1. Get out of _____ , Fred!

2. Will you _____ me in?

3. Ben has _____ pet ducks.

4. Will you _____ that bug away from me?

5. _____ , I will hop with you.

6. Jeff likes the _____ cap best.

Spiral Review

A complete sentence has two parts.
It tells who or what did something.
It also tells what someone or something
does or did.

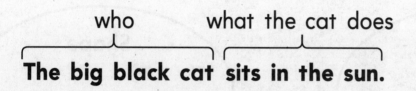

who   what the cat does

The big black cat sits in the sun.

Draw a line under each group of words
that is a complete sentence.

1. My dog ate its food.

2. The bus came late.

3. eat lunch at school

4. the girls in my class

5. Our family went to the park.

Planning My Description

Listen to the labels in the web and read along. Write and draw details that tell size, shape, color, and number.

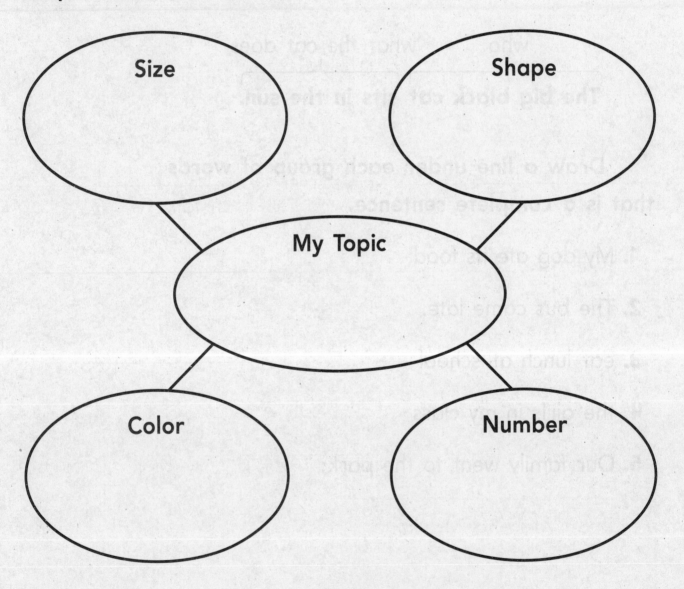

Grammar in Writing

Some **nouns** name **one**. Some nouns name more than one.

An **s** ending means more than one. Some special nouns change their spelling to name more than one.

✏️ Listen to the sentences and read along. Fix the mistakes in these statements. Use proofreading marks.

    Examples: I read three ~~book~~ books. Two ~~man~~ men talk.

1. One dogs swims.

2. Two elephant drink water.

3. Three woman eat cake.

4. Many bell ring.

Proofreading Marks	
∧	add
⌿	take out

Final Blends

✏️ Name each picture. Write the letters that stand for the ending sounds. Use the letters from the box.

| nd | mp | nt | st | sk |

1.

_ _ _ _ _

2.

_ _ _ _ _

3.

_ _ _ _ _

4.

_ _ _ _ _

5.

_ _ _ _ _

6.

_ _ _ _ _

Name _____

Words to Know

✏️ Write a word from the box to complete each sentence. Use the leftover word to write a sentence.

> ## Words to Know
>
> | eat | give | one |
> |-----|------|-----|
> | put | small | take |

_____

1. Liz will _____ Ken a box.

2. He will _____ a snack.

3. I can see _____ duck.

4. The ant is _____.

5. Jill will _____ the truck away.

_____

_____

135

Name _____

Final Blends

Name each picture. Circle the word to finish the sentence.

1.

Fran has a ____ .

list   gift

2.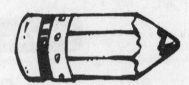

You can ____ with this.

grasp   print

3.

Ann plays in the ____ .

sand   dust

4.

It can ____ up.

land   jump

5.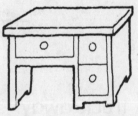

Do you sit at a ____?

desk   pond

6.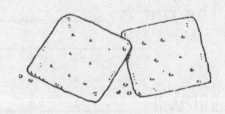

These can be very ____ .

stand   crisp

Spelling Words with the Short *u* Sound

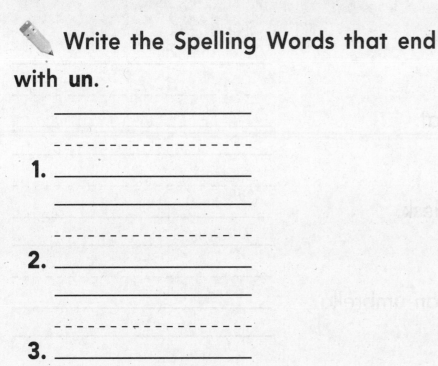 Write the Spelling Words that end with **un**.

_____

1. _____

_____

2. _____

_____

3. _____

Spelling Words

us

sun

but

fun

bus

run

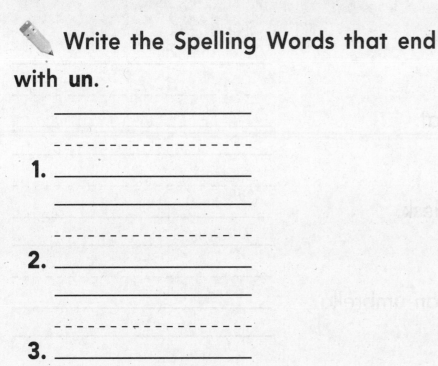 Write the Spelling Words that end with **us**.

_____   _____

4. _____   5. _____

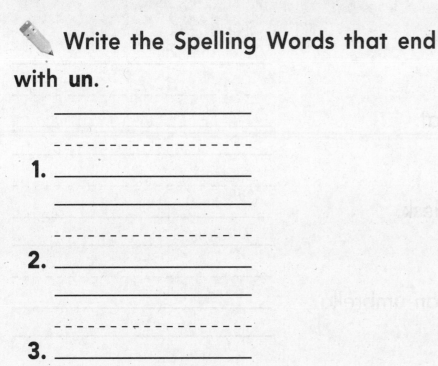 Write the Spelling Word that ends with **ut**.

_____

6. _____

Articles

 Circle the article in each sentence.
Write it on the line.

1. The gift was a hat.

2. Nan sat at the desk.

3. We stand under an umbrella.

4. The dogs ate fast.

**Circle the article that belongs in
each sentence.**

5. Nan sat on (an, the) steps.

6. He put his bag on (a, an) chair.

Writing a Topic Sentence

 Look at the picture of Stan the Skunk.
Tell what Stan looks like. Write a topic
sentence and some details.

Topic Sentence:

_____

- -

_____

- -

He has a _____ .

_____

- -

He has _____ .

Short *u* and Final Blends

✏️ Name each picture. Write the last two consonants that stand for the sounds at the end of the word. Choose consonants from the box.

lp	nt	mp	ft	sk

1.

ju _____

2.

a _____

3.

he _____

4.

so _____

5.

bu _____

6.

ma _____

A Cupcake Party

Please and Thank You

Read pages 144–149. Help Fritz make a party invitation to give to his friends. Use details from the story to tell about the party.

Please come to my cupcake party!

Where: Fritz's house

When: Today!

What we will do:

_____

_____ •

_____ •

_____

_____

_____ •

_____ •

Read pages 150–157. Then be one of Fritz's friends. Write a thank-you note to Fritz. Tell what you liked about the party.

Dear Fritz,

_____

- -

_____

_____

_____

_____

- -

_____

Love,

_____

- -

_____

Name _____

Spelling Words with the Short *u* Sound

✏️ Write the missing letter to complete each Spelling Word. Then write the word.

Spelling Words
us
sun
but
fun
bus
run

1. b ___ t _____

2. s ___ n _____

3. ___ s _____

4. f ___ n _____

5. b ___ s _____

6. r ___ n _____

Articles

Listen to each sentence. Read along.
Circle the article that belongs in each sentence.

1. We went on (a, an) ride.

2. She read about (a, an) elephant.

3. The bear ate (a, the) berries.

4. Bill ate (a, an) orange.

5. I know (the, a) answer.

6. They found (a, an) nest.

Spelling Words with the Short *u* Sound

 Write a Spelling Word to complete each sentence.

_____
- - - - - - - - - - - - - - - -

1. Here comes the _____ .

_____
- - - - - - - - - - - - - -

2. The _____ is up.

_____
- - - - - - - - - - - - - -

3. The dog can _____ fast.

 Write the correct word to complete each sentence.

_____
- - - - - - - - - - - - - - - -

us

4. Will you come with _____ ?

is

_____
- - - - - - - - - - - - - -

fun

5. We had a lot of _____ .

fan

_____
- - - - - - - - - - - - - -

bat

6. I like black _____ not red.

but

Spiral Review

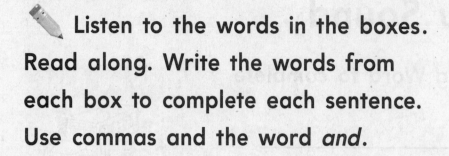 Listen to the words in the boxes.
Read along. Write the words from
each box to complete each sentence.
Use commas and the word *and*.

| dogs   cats   birds |

1. We have _____

| sing   dance   act |

2. The girl can _____

| apples   plums   pears |

3. He eats _____

Grammar in Writing

✏️ Write each sentence. Use the article from the Word Bank that belongs in each sentence.

Word Bank

a

an

the

1. My friend has _____ apple.

_____

- -

_____

2. I saw _____ otter at the zoo.

_____

- -

_____

3. The boy has _____ gifts.

_____

- -

_____

From Seed to Pumpkin

My Seed Packet

Make your own pumpkin seed packet.

First, draw a pumpkin plant on the front.

Pumpkin Seeds

Write about how to grow pumpkins on the back of your packet. Choose words from the box to complete the sentences.

| seedlings shoots seeds water flowers |

How to Grow a Pumpkin

_____

- - - - - - - - - - - - - - - - - - - -

1. First, plant the _____ in soil.

_____

- - - - - - - - - - - - - - - - - - - -

2. In two weeks, green _____ come up.

_____

- - - - - - - - - - - - - - - - - - - -

3. Next, they grow into _____.

_____

- - - - - - - - - - - - - - - - - - - -

4. Be sure to give your plant _____.

_____

- - - - - - - - - - - - - - - - - - - -

5. In summer, orange _____ bloom on your plants.

6. In fall, you will have big orange pumpkins!

Words with *th*

 Circle the word that matches the picture.

1.

wind   with

2.

tan   thin

3.

them   ten

4.

bat   bath

5.

path   pet

6.

kick   thick

Name _____

Lesson 11
READER'S NOTEBOOK

At Home in the Ocean
High-Frequency Words

Words to Know

✏️ **Listen to the riddles. Read along.**
Circle the best answer to each riddle.

1. This is a place that is not near. **far** **where** **live**

2. This is how snow feels. **their** **blue** **cold**

3. This word could start a question. **far** **where** **live**

4. A rock does not do this. **cold** **where** **live**

5. Rain is made of this. **water** **far** **cold**

6. The sky is this. **where** **blue** **little**

7. This is not big. **water** **little** **far**

8. This belongs to more than one person. **their** **water** **far**

Words with *th*

✏️ Write **th** to finish the word and read it.
Circle the picture that matches the word.

1.

$1 + 1 = 2$

m a __ __ __

2.

__ __ i n k

3.

__ __ i c k

4.

b a __ __

5.

__ __ i s

Spelling Words with the *th* Sound

✏ Sort the words. Write the correct Spelling Words in each column.

Words that begin with **th**	Words that end with **th**
_____	_____
- - - - - - - - -	- - - - - - - - -
_____	_____
_____	_____
- - - - - - - - -	- - - - - - - - -
_____	_____
_____	_____
- - - - - - - - -	- - - - - - - - -
_____	_____
_____	_____
- - - - - - - - -	- - - - - - - - -
_____	_____

Spelling Words

that

then

this

them

with

bath

Names for People, Animals, Places, and Things

✏️ Circle each proper noun that names a special person or animal.

1. My friend Kim sees a crab.

2. Stan Bock sees it, too.

3. They call the crab Fred.

✏️ Circle each proper noun that names a special place or thing.

4. We went to the Carson Zoo.

5. We walked from Brown Avenue.

6. My favorite show was Talking Birds.

Name _____

Words That Tell How

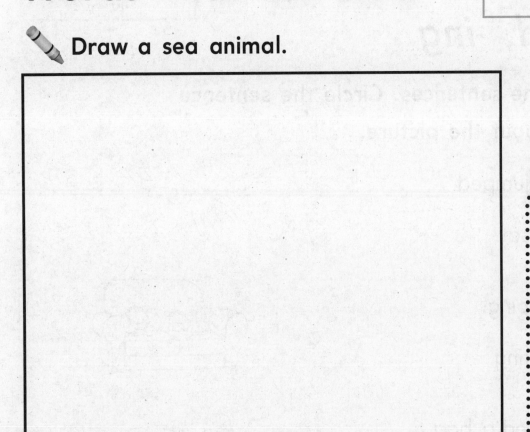 Draw a sea animal.

Word Bank

softly
loudly
slowly
quickly
fast
happily
sadly
sleepily
gently

Write sentences about your animal. Listen to the words in the box. Use these words and other words you choose.

Sea Animal	Action Verb	How

Sea Animal	Action Verb	How

Base Words and -*s*, -*es*, -*ed*, -*ing*

✏️ Read the sentences. Circle the sentence that tells about the picture.

1. The cat jumped.

The cat sat.

2. He is helping.

He is resting.

3. She packed a bag.

She pulled a bag.

4. Meg calls her pet.

Meg pets her cat.

5. Val is drawing.

Val is looking.

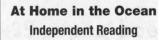

Reader's Guide

At Home in the Ocean
Interesting Animals

Read pages 16–21. Draw an ocean animal you learned about. Write why it is interesting.

_____

- -

_____

- -

_____

Read pages 22–29. Draw another ocean animal. Write why it is interesting.

_____

- -

_____

- -

_____

- .

Spelling Words with the *th* Sound

✏️ Listen to the clues. Read along. Write the Spelling Word that fits each clue.

Spelling Words

that
then
this
them
with
bath

1. Rhymes with **cat** _____

2. Rhymes with **path** _____

3. Rhymes with **hen** _____

4. Rhymes with **miss** _____

5. Rhymes with **hem** _____

6. Completes this sentence:
I go ____ you. _____

Lesson 11
READER'S NOTEBOOK

Titles for People

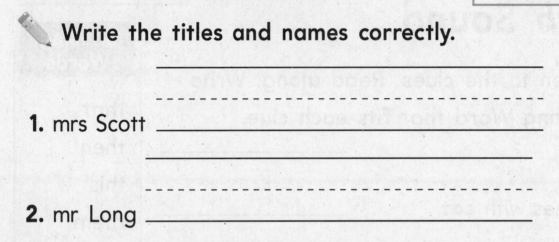 Write the titles and names correctly.

_____

_ _

1. mrs Scott _____

_____

_ _

2. mr Long _____

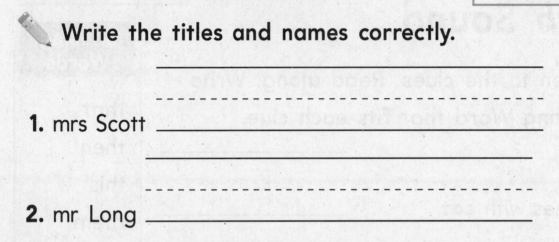 Draw a line under each title. Then write the title and name correctly.

3. Today miss Hill will play the drums.

_____

_ _

_____

4. Can dr Well fix the dog's leg?

_____

_ _

_____

5. ms. Hass takes a picture of the class.

_____

_ _

_____

Planning My Sentences

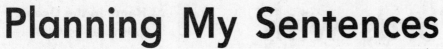 Write and draw facts about your sea animal.

My Topic

Fact 1

Fact 2

Spelling Words with the *th* Sound

✎ Write a Spelling Word from the box to complete each sentence.

Spelling Words

that

bath

them

_____

- - - - - - - - - - - - -

1. _____ hat is for Jack.

_____

- - - - - - - - - - - - -

2. Tell _____ to come in now.

_____

- - - - - - - - - - - - -

3. I like to give my dog a _____ .

✎ Write a Spelling Word from the box to complete each sentence.

Spelling Words

then

this

with

_____

- - - - - - - - - - - - -

4. _____ Jon was up at bat.

_____

- - - - - - - - - - - - -

5. Matt, is _____ your hat?

_____

- - - - - - - - - - - - -

6. Sam went swimming _____ me.

Spiral Review

✏️ Draw a line under the possessive noun(s) in each sentence.

1. The girl's bike is red.

2. We found Dad's hat.

3. I like Jose's story.

4. The cat's tail is long.

5. This is Miss Linn's book.

Grammar in Writing

Nouns that name special people, animals, places, or things are called **proper nouns**. Proper nouns begin with capital letters.

A **title** before a person's name begins with a capital letter. A title usually ends with a period.

✏️ **Fix the mistakes in these statements. Use proofreading marks.**

Examples: My fish is named gus.

I gave Mrs Billows a book.

We went to storytime at carter library.

1. My friend dr Rudd helps animals.

2. He has a pet crab called pinch.

3. Our teacher took us to see the liberty bell.

4. We visited the grand canyon.

Proofreading Marks	
∧	add
≡	capital letter

Words with *ch*, *tch*

 Circle the word that matches the picture.

1.

thick   chick

2.

chip   champ

3.

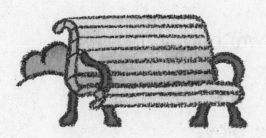

bend   bench

4.

hatch   hut

5.

chin   check

6.

cats   catch

Grade 1, Unit 3

Name _____

Lesson 12
READER'S NOTEBOOK

How Leopard Got
His Spots
High-Frequency Words

Words to Know

✏️ Circle the word that best completes each sentence.

1. The dog is (brown, very).

2. Rich got the gift (been, out) of the box.

3. I would like to have my (never, own) cat.

4. Singing makes me (very, brown) happy.

5. Have you (know, been) to the play?

6. Do you (know, very) what to do next?

7. Take (off, never) that hat.

8. You (own, never) sing with me.

Words with *ch*, *tch*

✏️ Read the words in the box. Write the word that matches the picture.

Word Bank

lunch   check   chimp   chop   match

1. _____

2. _____

3. _____

4. _____

5.  _____

Spelling Words with the *ch* Sound

Sort the words. Write the correct Spelling Words in each column.

Spelling Words

chin
chop
much
chip
rich
chick

Words that begin with **ch**	Words that end with **ch**

Commands

 Draw a line under each command.

1. Come when I call you.

2. I will call you soon.

3. Run around the track.

4. She can run fast.

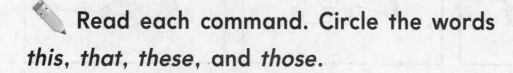 **Read each command. Circle the words** *this*, *that*, *these*, **and** *those*.

5. Tell those children to come.

6. Eat this apple.

7. Bring me that picture.

8. Sit on these chairs.

Order Words

 Write 1, 2, and 3 to put these pictures in order.

 Write instructions that tell how to feed a cat. Use order words.

Order Word	Action	Thing
Order Word	Action	Thing
Order Word	Action	Thing

Possessives with *'s*

🖊️ **Read the sentences. Circle the sentence that tells about the picture.**

1. Mom's hat is off!

   Dad's hat is wet.

2. My cat's leg is cut.

   My cat's bed is small.

3. Meg's bag is big.

   Peg's bag is little.

4. Tim's picture is cold.

   Tom's picture is funny.

5. My pal's pet is wet.

   The vet is my pet's friend.

Name _____   Date _____

Lesson 12
READER'S NOTEBOOK

How Leopard Got
His Spots
Independent Reading

How Leopard Got His Spots

Before and After

Read pages 48–59. Draw
one of Fred's friends. What did the friend
look like before and after Fred painted it?
Then write a word to describe the animal
before and after.

Before

After

_____

- - - - - - - - - - - - - -

_____

Name _____ Date _____

Lesson 12
READER'S NOTEBOOK

How Leopard Got
His Spots
Independent Reading

Read pages 60–63. Draw a picture of Hal with his new paint job. How do you think Hal feels? Write what Hal might say to Fred.

Spelling Words with *ch*

Listen to the clues. Read along. Write
the Spelling Word that fits each clue.

**Spelling
Words**

chin

chop

much

chip

rich

chick

1. Opposite of **poor**

2. Rhymes with **hop**

3. Rhymes with **fin**

4. Opposite of **little**

5. Rhymes with **hip**

6. Rhymes with **kick**

Commands

 Draw a line under each command.

1. We ate dinner.

2. Eat your dinner.

3. Have a snack.

4. She had a snack.

 Write each command to show strong feeling.

5. Wait for me.

_____

- -

_____

6. Hurry up.

_____

- -

_____

Name _____

Lesson 12
READER'S NOTEBOOK

How Leopard Got
His Spots
Writing: Informative Writing

Planning My Instructions

✏️ Write steps for making an animal puppet. Write the steps in order. Use an order word for each step.

_____
- -

My Topic: How to _____

1. _____

2. _____

3. _____

4. _____

Spelling Words with the *ch* Sound

✏️ Write the correct word to complete each sentence.

_____

1. Jan rubs her _____ .

chin

fin

_____

2. The _____ is small and soft.

chick

check

_____

3. How _____ does it cost?

chum

much

_____

4. Dad will _____ the nuts.

chop

chat

_____

5. There is a _____ in the cup.

ship

chip

_____

6. The king was very _____ .

rich

rip

Spiral Review

Listen to the animal names in the Word Bank. Read along. Draw lines to match naming parts and action parts. Your sentence should tell about the picture.

Word Bank

zebras   giraffe   turtle

1. The zebras   is hot.

2. A giraffe   drink water.

3. The turtle   has a snack.

4. The sun   takes a swim.

Write an action part to make a sentence.

5. The animals _____ .

Name _____

Lesson 12
READER'S NOTEBOOK

How Leopard Got
His Spots
Grammar: Commands

Grammar in Writing

Commands are simple sentences that tell someone to do something. A simple command begins with a **capital letter** and ends with a **period**.

✏️ **Fix the mistakes in these commands. Use proofreading marks.**

Example: w̲ait for me ⊙

1. feed the giraffe

2. paint a new sign

3. pick up your brush

4. read us this story

Proofreading Marks	
≡	capital letter
⊙	period

Words with *sh*, *wh*, *ph*

✏️ Circle the word that matches the picture or belongs in the sentence.

1.

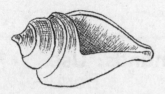

shell   bell

2.

_____
- - - - - -
_____ is this?

What   Wish

3.

_____
- - - - - -
_____ will he go?

Well   When

4.

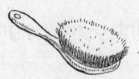

bunch   brush

5.

fish   fist

6.

Ralph   Jen

Words to Know

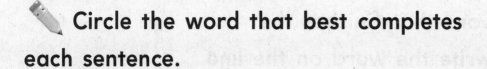 **Circle the word that best completes each sentence.**

1. Some frogs are (green, grow).

2. Let us have lunch (yellow, down) by the pond.

3. It gets cold in the (fall, new).

4. My plants will (down, grow) well in the sun.

5. Some of the buds are (goes, open).

6. Do you like my (new, down) hat?

7. A big (yellow, fall) truck will take the logs away.

8. The truck (green, goes) to the dump.

Words with *sh*, *wh*, *ph*

✏ Circle the word that finishes the sentence. Then write the word on the line.

1.

wish
witch

_____

I _____ I had a pet dog.

2.

pin
ship

_____

The _____ was in the water.

3.

where
her

_____

Do you know _____ she is?

4.

Then
When

_____

_____ will the shop open?

5.

tan
graph

_____

Dan will draw a math _____.

Spelling Words with the *sh* and *wh* Sounds

✏️ Sort the words. Write the correct Spelling Words in each column.

Words with **sh**	Words with **wh**
_____	_____
_____	_____
_____	_____
_____	_____

Spelling Words

ship

shop

which

when

whip

fish

✏️ Write two words that rhyme with **lip**.

_____   _____

_____   _____

Name _____

Lesson 13
READER'S NOTEBOOK

Seasons
Grammar: Subjects
and Verbs

Subjects and Verbs

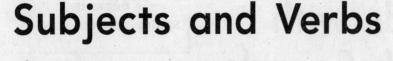 Write a verb from the box to tell what the underlined subject is doing.

_____
- - - - - - - - - - - - - - - - - - -

1. The <u>sun</u> _____ up.

2. <u>Bev</u> _____ on the sand.

3. The <u>girls</u> _____ up sticks.

4. A <u>frog</u> _____ past.

5. The <u>dogs</u> _____ after the rabbits.

Word Bank

pick

hops

sits

run

comes

Main Idea

✏️ Write facts to finish three sentences about a season. Then tell the main idea.

| Topic Sentence |

_____
- - - - - - - - - - - - - - -

Here are some facts about _____ .

| Detail Sentence |

_____   _____
- - - - - - - - - - - -   - - - - - - - - - - - - -

_____ is a time when _____
_____
- -

_____

| Detail Sentence |

_____
- - - - - - - - - - -

The weather in _____ gets

_____
- -

_____

| Main Idea |

_____
- - - - - - - - - - -

All my sentences tell about _____ .

Contractions with *'s, n't*

✏️ Draw a line from each pair of words to its contraction.

can not   don't

Let us   It's

do not   can't

It is   Let's

Write the contraction from above that finishes each sentence.

_____

_____

1. They _____ know what to do.

_____

_____

2. _____ good to help a friend.

_____

_____

3. _____ go to see a play.

_____

_____

4. He _____ find his hat.

Name _____ Date _____

Reader's Guide

Seasons

Our Seasons

Read pages 82–85. What is important about spring? Draw and write about it.

> **Spring**

_____

- -

_____

_____

- -

_____

_____

- -

_____

Read pages 86–89. What is important about summer? Draw and write about it.

Summer

_____

- -

_____

- -

_____

Read pages 90–97. What is important about fall or winter? Draw and write about it.

_____

- -

_____

- -

_____

Name _____

Spelling Words with the *sh* and *wh* Sounds

✏️ Write **sh** or **wh** to complete each Spelling Word.

Spelling Words

ship
shop
which
when
whip
fish

1.

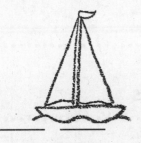

___ ___ i p

2.

f i ___ ___

3.

___ ___ o p

4.

___ ___ i c h

5.

___ ___ e n

6.

___ ___ i p

Name _____

Verbs with *s*

✏️ Listen to the nouns in the Word Bank and read along. Choose the correct verb to agree with the underlined subject. Write the verb to finish each sentence.

Word Bank

children   boy   girls

_____

1. Many <u>children</u> _____ by the pond.

play   plays

_____

2. A <u>boy</u> _____ in the water.

jump   jumps

_____

3. The <u>girls</u> _____ the ball.

hit   hits

_____

4. A <u>boy and a dog</u> _____ on the sand.

run   runs

Planning My Sentences

✏️ Choose a season. Then write facts about the season.

My Topic: _____

Fact 1

Fact 2

Fact 3

Closing Sentence

Spelling Words with
sh, *wh*, *ph*

✏️ Write the correct word to complete
each sentence.

_____

- - - - - - - - - - - - - - - -

1. The _____ has left. (shell, ship, chip)

_____

- - - - - - - - - - - - - - - -

2. _____ way did he go? (Which, Why, Who)

_____

- - - - - - - - - - - - - - - -

3. The _____ sells hats. (chop, shop, she)

_____

- - - - - - - - - - - - - - - -

4. _____ will you go? (Where, Went, When)

_____

- - - - - - - - - - - - - - - -

5. Can you _____ the eggs? (win, why, whip)

_____

- - - - - - - - - - - - - - - -

6. The _____ are yellow. (dash, fish, dish)

Spiral Review

✏️ Draw lines to match naming parts and action parts. Read the statements you made about the picture.

1. Jill   waters the plants.

2. Fred   takes a nap.

3. The mom   digs in the mud.

4. The dad   is looking.

5. The cat   holds a box of plants.

✏️ Choose one statement. Write it, adding adjectives or other details.

_____

- -

6. _____

Name _____

Lesson 13
READER'S NOTEBOOK

Seasons
Grammar: Subjects
and Verbs

Grammar in Writing

- Add **s** to a **verb** when it tells about a noun that names one.
- Do not add **s** to a verb when it tells about a noun that names more than one.

✏️ **Fix the mistakes in these sentences.**
Use proofreading marks.

Examples: Snowflakes f̶a̶l̶l̶s̶ ^**fall** on the ground.

David p̶u̶t̶ ^**puts** on his coat.

1. Don get his sled.

2. Jan and Nick plays in the sand.

3. Nick make a hill of sand.

4. The dog jump in the grass.

5. Deb and Don finds a cat.

Proofreading Marks	
∧	add
⟋	take out

Words with Long *a*

Circle the word that matches the picture.

1.

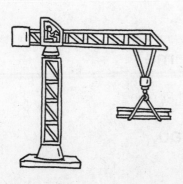

camp   crane

2.

plane   plan

3.

crack   cake

4.

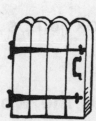

grass   gate

5.

whale   what

6.

vest   vase

Words to Know

✏️ Circle the word that best completes each sentence.

1. Can you (watch/into) my fish for me?

2. I will go (into/starts) class with you.

3. I am glad that lunch (watch/starts) at one.

4. The fox jumps (over/watch) the log.

✏️ Write the word for each number.

2 _____

3 _____

4 _____

5 _____

Words to Know

five

four

three

two

Words with Long *a*

✏️ Write the word that goes with each clue.

Word Bank

- plate
- tape
- male
- skates
- game
- grape

1. You use this to close a box.

_____

2. A man is this.

_____

3. You eat from this.

_____

4. Go fast on these.

_____

5. This is little and can be green.

_____

6. You play this with a friend.

_____

Spelling Words with the Long *a* Sound

 Write the Spelling Words in ABC order.

Spelling Words
came
make
brave
late
gave
shape

_____

1. _____

2. _____

3. _____

4. _____

5. _____

6. _____

Name _____

Verbs with *ed*

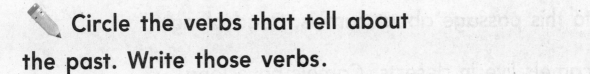 Circle the verbs that tell about the past. Write those verbs.

_____
- - - - - - - - - - - - - - - - - -
1. The game _____ at one.

starts   started

_____
- - - - - - - - - - - - - - - - - -
2. Stan _____ the box.

fills   filled

_____
- - - - - - - - - - - - - - - - - -
3. Jane _____ at the pictures.

looks   looked

_____
- - - - - - - - - - - - - - - - - -
4. The frog _____ very far.

jumps   jumped

_____
- - - - - - - - - - - - - - - - - -
5. Mr. Scott _____ the best one.

picks   picked

Taking Notes

Listen to this passage about camels. Read along.

Many camels live in deserts. Camels have long legs and humps on their backs. Camels can live to be 50 or even 60 years old. Camels eat plants that grow in the desert.

Take notes about camels. Use words and pictures. Put your notes in the correct boxes.

Bodies

How Long They Live

Food

Words with Soft *c, g, dge*

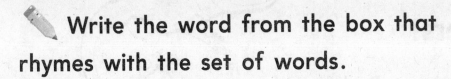 Write the word from the box that rhymes with the set of words.

Word Bank

face
gem
page
cell
judge
wedge

1. fudge   nudge   budge   _____

2. cage   wage   rage   _____

3. race   lace   pace   _____

4. them   hem   stem   _____

5. tell   bell   yell   _____

6. edge   ledge   hedge   _____

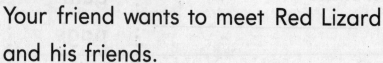

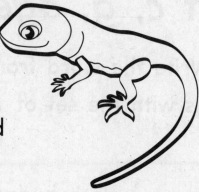

The Big Race

Meet the Racers!

Your friend wants to meet Red Lizard
and his friends.

**Read pages 126–128. What do you know
about Red Lizard?**

_____

- -

_____ .

Read page 129. Tell about Cottontail.

_____

- -

_____

_____ .

Read page 130. What do you know about Rat?

_____

- -

_____ .

Name _____ Date _____

Read pages 131–136. What do you know about Snake?

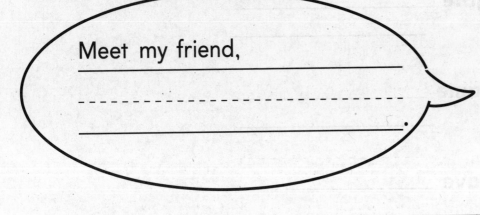

_____

- - - - - - - - - - - - - - - - - - -

_____.

Read page 137. Tell about Roadrunner.

_____

- -

_____.

Read pages 138–143. Pick one character to introduce to your friend. Tell important things about the character.

Meet my friend,
_____

- - - - - - - - - - - - - - - - -

_____.

_____

- - - - - - - - - - - - - - - - - - - -

_____

_____

- - - - - - - - - - - - - - - - - - - -

_____

_____

Spelling Words with the Long *a* Sound

Listen to the clues. Read along. Write the Spelling Word that fits each clue.

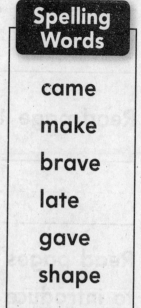

Spelling Words

came
make
brave
late
gave
shape

_____

1. Rhymes with **tape** _____

_____

2. Opposite of **afraid** _____

_____

3. Rhymes with **gate** _____

_____

4. Rhymes with **tame** _____

_____

5. Rhymes with **cave** _____

_____

6. Rhymes with **bake** _____

Present and Past Time

Listen to the time words in the Word Bank. Read along. Circle the correct verb to show present or past time. Write it on the line.

Word Bank

now   today   yesterday

_____

- - - - - - - - - - - - - - - - - -

1. Meg _____ at the clock now.
(present time)

looks   looked

_____

- - - - - - - - - - - - - - - - - -

2. Today we _____ games for math.
(present time)

play   played

_____

- - - - - - - - - - - - - - - - - -

3. Yesterday Ron _____ his dad make

lunch. (past time)

help   helped

Spelling Words with the Long *a* Sound

✏️ Write a Spelling Word from the box to complete each sentence.

Spelling Words

came
late
make
brave
shape
gave

1. I got here _____.

2. Will you _____ me a cake?

3. He _____ to play with me.

4. Max is big and _____.

5. He _____ me a new pen.

6. What _____ is that box?

Spiral Review

Listen to the nouns. Read along. Circle the correct noun to name each picture. Then write the noun.

1.    prize   prizes   _____

2.   child   children   _____

3.    woman   women   _____

 Finish the sentence with the correct verb.

_____

4. Plants _____ water to grow.

    needs   **need**

_____

5. A camel _____ desert plants.

    eat   **eats**

Planning My Report

The Big Race
Writing: Informative Writing

✏️ Write a question about the animal you choose. Then find and write facts to answer your question.

_____

- - - - - - - - - - - - - - - - - - -

My Topic: _____

My Question

Fact 1

Fact 2

Fact 3

Grammar in Writing

- Some verbs tell what is happening now. Some verbs tell what happened in the past.
- Add **ed** to most verbs to tell about the past.

✎ **Listen to the time words in the Word Bank. Read along. Fix the mistakes in these sentences. Use proofreading marks.**

> **Word Bank**
>
> now   yesterday   last night

                              watched
Examples: Many people ~~watch~~ the race
                           ∧
last night.

1. The animals played now.

2. The frog and snake talk yesterday.

3. Last night the rat visits the duck.

Proofreading Marks	
∧	add
℘	take out

Words with Long *i*

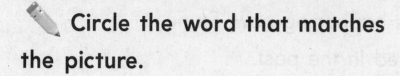 Circle the word that matches the picture.

1.

bake   bike

2.

dime   dim

3.

print   prize

4.

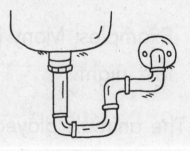

pale   pipe

5.

miss   mice

6.

hive   have

Words to Know

✏️ Circle the correct word to complete each sentence.

1. Lan goes for a (walk, bird) in the park.

2. It is a very (both, long) path.

3. Lan sees a (or, bird) in its nest.

4. Will it (fly, long) away when it sees her?

5. Two ducks in the lake are (bird, both) wet.

6. Their (eyes, walk) are black.

7. Lan likes to watch (those, eyes) ducks.

8. Lan has to go now (fly, or) she will be late.

Words with Long *i*

Write the word that best completes each sentence. Use words from the Word Bank.

Word Bank

- time
- smile
- ride
- like
- kite

_____

- - - - - - - - - - - - - - - - -

1. Pat and I _____ to play.

_____

- - - - - - - - - - - - - - - - -

2. Pat likes to _____ her bike.

_____

- - - - - - - - - - - - - - - - -

3. I like to fly my _____ .

_____

- - - - - - - - - - - - - - - - -

4. Pat is fun. She makes me _____ .

_____

- - - - - - - - - - - - - - - - -

5. We have a good _____ .

Spelling Words with the Long *i* Sound

Look at the picture. Write the missing letter to complete each Spelling Word.

Spelling Words

drive
time
bike
white
kite
like

1.

t __ m e

2.

l __ k e

3.

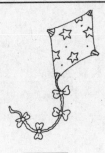

k __ t e

4.

b __ k e

5.

wh __ t e

6.

dr __ v e

Using *is* and *are*

Circle **is** or **are** to finish each sentence.
Then write those verbs.

_____

- - - - - - - - - - - - - - - - -

1. The eyes _____ blue.

is   **are**

_____

- - - - - - - - - - - - - - - - -

2. The snake _____ thin.

is   **are**

_____

- - - - - - - - - - - - - - - - -

3. The chicks _____ soft.

is   **are**

_____

- - - - - - - - - - - - - - - - -

4. The mice _____ very little.

is   **are**

_____

- - - - - - - - - - - - - - - - -

5. The egg _____ small.

is   **are**

Using Clear Words

Listen to the animal names. Read along. Make the meaning of each sentence clearer. Write new words to take the place of the underlined word or words.

1.	A giraffe is <u>big</u>.
	A giraffe is
	_____
	- - - - - - - - - - - - - -
	_____.

2.	Puppies can <u>play</u>.
	Puppies can
	_____
	- - - - - - - - - - - - - -
	_____.

3.	Squirrels can go up <u>tall things</u>.
	Squirrels can go up
	_____
	- - - - - - - - - - - - - -
	_____.

Digraphs *kn, wr, gn, mb*

✏️ Circle the two words in each row that begin or end with the same sound. Write the letters that stand for the sound.

kn	wr	gn	mb

1.	wrap	white	wrist
2.	lamb	numb	crab
3.	kite	knot	knack
4.	grape	gnash	gnat
5.	write	water	wren
6.	knife	knit	kick

**Reader's Guide**

Animal Groups

What Is an Animal?

Make your own diagram. Look at **Animal Groups** for an example.

Read pages 166–172. Then draw a turtle.
Add labels: scales, tail, eye, legs, shell.

Read pages 173–183. Draw a picture of yourself. Add these labels: hair, eyes, mouth, legs. Add more labels.

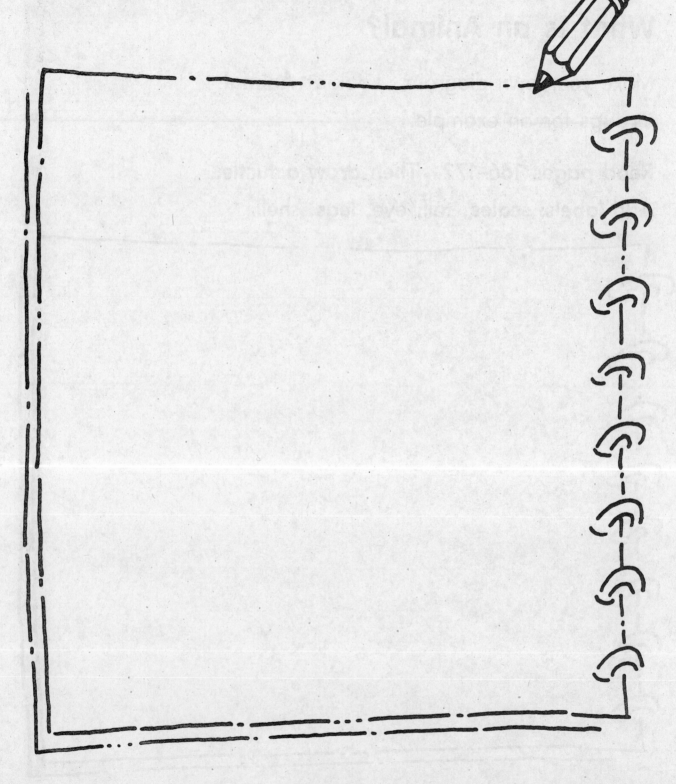

Name _____

Spelling Words with the Long *i* Sound

✏️ Write the Spelling Words that rhyme with **hike.**

_____   _____

1. _____   2. _____

✏️ Write the Spelling Words that rhyme with **bite.**

_____   _____

3. _____   4. _____

✏️ Write the Spelling Word that rhymes with **dime.**

_____

5. _____

✏️ Write the Spelling Word that rhymes with **hive.**

_____

6. _____

Spelling Words

time
like
kite
bike
white
drive

Using *was* and *were*

✏️ Circle **was** or **were** to finish each sentence. Then write the verb on the line.

_____

1. The cat _____ napping.

   was   **were**

_____

2. The ducks _____ in the pond.

   was   **were**

_____

3. The pigs _____ in their pen.

   was   **were**

_____

4. The snake _____ on the grass.

   was   **were**

_____

5. The frogs _____ in the water.

   was   **were**

Spelling Words with the Long *i* Sound

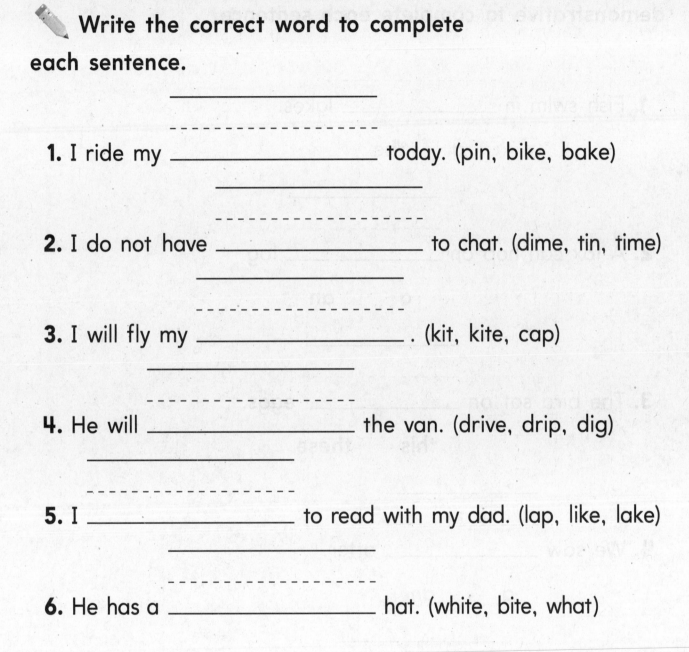 Write the correct word to complete each sentence.

_____
- - - - - - - - - - - - - - -

1. I ride my _____ today. (pin, bike, bake)

_____
- - - - - - - - - - - - - - -

2. I do not have _____ to chat. (dime, tin, time)

_____
- - - - - - - - - - - - - - -

3. I will fly my _____ . (kit, kite, cap)

_____
- - - - - - - - - - - - - - -

4. He will _____ the van. (drive, drip, dig)

_____
- - - - - - - - - - - - - - -

5. I _____ to read with my dad. (lap, like, lake)

_____
- - - - - - - - - - - - - - -

6. He has a _____ hat. (white, bite, what)

Spiral Review

✏️ Write the correct article or demonstrative to complete each sentence.

```
     _____
     - - - - - - - - -
```

1. Fish swim in _____ lakes.

a   the

```
        _____
        - - - - - - - -
```

2. A fox can hop on _____ log.

a   an

```
        _____
        - - - - - - - -
```

3. The bird sat on _____ eggs.

this   these

```
     _____
     - - - - - - - - -
```

4. We saw _____ otter.

a   an

```
     _____
     - - - - - - - - -
```

5. The frog ate _____ bug.

that   those

Grammar in Writing

- The verbs **is** and **are** tell what is happening now. The verbs **was** and **were** tell what happened in the past.
- Use **is** or **was** with a noun that names one.

✏️ **Fix the mistakes in these sentences.**
Use proofreading marks.

Example: Frogs ~~was~~ once tadpoles. A frog
⌃were
~~are~~ small.
⌃is

1. Cats is mammals.

2. Dogs was once pups.

3. The fox were once a cub.

4. Apes is strong.

Proofreading Marks	
⌃	add
و	take out